A Guide to Love, Dating and Purity

God's way.

Trish I. Castlen

Edited by: Steve A. Castlen

Cover design by: Kelly B. Castlen

ISBN: 978-1975990176

Contents

Introduction: The Maze..5

Chapter 1
Benefits of involving God in our lives................................9

Chapter 2
Do I consult God or follow my heart?............................25

Chapter 3
Different ways that God talk to us...................................31

Chapter 4
To be guided by God you must...49

Chapter 5
The protection of God..65

Chapter 6
It isn't difficult for God to bring two people together.........................71

Chapter 7
Purity..87

Chapter 8
Questions & Answers...101

Model prayer for your future partner.............................129

INTRODUCTION:

THE MAZE

Life can feel like a maze. Not always the fun kind like on the back of a cereal box. Sometimes it's the scary one in the movies. You know the ones. The main character ends up in an elaborate labyrinth where one wrong turn could be fatal. There are traps, dark areas, obstacles, dangers, dead ends, and unexpected twists. Never certain which path to take or what's coming around the next corner, the hero bravely pushes through and usually makes it out alive!

In real life, labyrinths come in different forms, but we still must navigate a series of complex pathways.
Major life decisions will take you down one path or another. How can we know if we are making good choices or not? How can we know where the hidden traps and dead ends are? How do we even know what lies at the end of the maze?

If life as a whole is like a labyrinth, then the search for a marriage partner is in itself a maze! Few choices are more important than this.

Who you marry affects the entire course of your future. It's easy to see the results of bad choices all around. Failed marriages are tragic and far too common. Nobody wants to choose poorly, and so the weight of such an important choice can seem overwhelming; even as disorienting and confusing as being in a real life maze! But according to God, for followers of Christ, things should be different.

Why does navigating the labyrinth of life bring so much fear, anxiety, frustration and pain? It seems to me that the biggest reason is our vantage point. We are looking at the journey exclusively from a grounded perspective; from below. The good news is there is another vantage point from above.

God created us and put us in this "maze". Some will immediately blame Him for the difficulties, disappointments, and frustrations of trying to make their way through the twists and turns of life.

What many have not realized is that God has provided a way for each individual to have a joyful and purposeful life; not just for those lucky enough to figure out the maze on their own.

He offers a guided path to everyone through the labyrinth of life's uncertainties. All we have to do is set our eyes on the One who created us and follow His lead.

As we come to God, we will realize that He was waiting for us with open arms and a map in hand. God has already provided what we need to live in abundance and victory in all areas, including our search for a spouse. Now He is just waiting for us to surrender our lives completely, so that He can guide us safely.

CHAPTER 1

Benefits of involving God in our lives

Benefits of involving God in our lives:

1-We have the guidance of a loving Father.

No one inside a maze can understand it. But looking at it from above would change things, wouldn't it?
God is the only one who can see the whole journey from above, so He knows exactly which path we should take. He is the perfect guide. Why pass up the ultimate advantage? In fact, He has already promised to lead us along the path we must follow, and teach us what we need to know along the way!

Read: Isaiah 48:17 and Acts 2:28

So many people's lives are like a walk in the dark through a maze of obstacles, traps, and unknown passages; having little idea where they are going. Their direction tends to be determined by how they feel in the moment rather than the knowledge of a reliable guide.

When you choose to involve God in your life, you will have extraordinary help and advantages. You will have a person on your side, who wants the best for you, who knows the geography ahead, who can warn you of dangers, and lead you through the good and the bad.

2-You will count on the light of Jesus and you will no longer walk in darkness.

Without God, people live in darkness, unaware of the benefits of a heavenly Guide! They are more likely to stumble, to go the wrong way, to expose themselves to unnecessary dangers, and disappointments. It is easy to see how depression or anxiety can take hold when we try it alone.

With God, (although at first glance we may not see much change) when we receive Him in our heart, we become citizens of a new kingdom. We leave the kingdom of darkness, and join the kingdom of light. We become children of God, children of light. Then we no longer live in the dark. We can see better and know where we're headed.

What a tremendous benefit, advantage, and blessing!

Read: Isaiah 60:1-3 and John 8:12

3- *You will have a reliable map.*

God has also provided a map to guide us: His Word, the Bible.
This is God's personal letter to us, with specific life instructions.
When you read this letter from your Heavenly Father with a humble attitude and follow it, you can experience a life of peace and victory. His letter to you will show you how to hear His directions and begin to develop godly wisdom.

What a great advantage it is to have in our hands the map of the Creator.

4- You will have divine help.

To his obedient children, God offers them:

-His protection (Read Psalm 91)

-His provision (Read Matthew 6: 25-34)

-His blessings (Read Deuteronomy 28:1-14)

-His miracles. God can display His power on your behalf (with healing, revelations, removing impossible barriers, miracles of all kinds, etc.)

Conclusion:

So think about it. If you had to go through a maze, wouldn't it be better to have a map in your hand and a wise and loving Father to guide you from above?
Suddenly, the journey doesn't sound so intimidating!

Unfortunately many do not want God to interfere in their lives. They dislike the idea of anyone telling them how to live.
Multitudes have refused God's offer of assistance, rejecting the map He has provided.

They forfeit the company and help of someone who knows the maze and loves them. They live in uncertainty and are vulnerable to dangers, traps, deceptions, mistakes, and their end will not be a happy one, because with each step they move further away from God. Only those who walk with God will be taken into His house in Heaven; a place He has prepared for those who love Him.

Decide today if you will surrender to the guidance of God.

 If you've realized that life is much better with God on your side and have decided to live with Him as your guide, then read the following:

You must first know that:

1-Every person who wants to have a relationship with God, must first repair the relationship that has been broken by sin.

The wrong you have done and the good that you have not done in the past has offended God. So the first step is:
Turn from your sins and ask for forgiveness from not only those sins, but for ignoring Him and His Word (The map).

2-To be able to approach God, your accounts with the Judge of the universe must be paid.

We have all sinned and disobeyed the moral laws of God, which deserves a punishment of death. The good news is that by dying on the cross, Jesus pays our debt to God and all who receive and believe in His name are given the power to be saved. The debt is canceled before God, you are clean in His eyes, and can begin a relationship without interference.

3-In order to live a life that pleases God, you have to decide to surrender to Him as your King (the one who's commands you will obey).

He is perfect, good and loving. To be under his rule and reign is the safest, most wonderful place to be. You must not wait until you are "good enough" to come to God. He gives you the strength to obey His commands. As you grow in this new relationship, you learn what pleases Him. His desires become your desires, you begin to love what He loves, and your decision making becomes God-centered. Your mind will be renewed because He is living in you! (Romans 12:2 and 1 Corinthians 3:16, 6:19)

4-We are all God's creation, but not all of us are His children.

God is waiting for you to receive Him as your heavenly Father. He loves you more than you can imagine.
He has a destiny and calling just for you. So position your heart to listen to His guidance, spend time with him each day in prayer, worshiping Him and reading His Word.

5- Knowledge must be followed by action.

Knowing that exercise is good for you is not enough. To appropriate the benefits you must exercise. To gain the benefit of that knowledge or information, you must act.

Many know about Jesus, and agree that He died long ago on a cross, but they have not received the benefit of that sacrifice. Mere knowledge of Jesus' death and resurrection will not guarantee them entrance to Heaven. Even the Devil himself believes Jesus died and rose again.

So, not only should you know that Jesus died on the cross in your place, but as an act of your will, you must place your trust in Him to receive that sacrifice. Put your faith in Jesus alone and surrender to Him as King and Lord of your life.

How do you receive the benefits of what Jesus did on the cross? With an action; a sincere prayer out loud.

Pray like this:

"Dear Father, I welcome you in my heart, I ask your forgiveness for my independence and for all the times I have offended you with my sins.

Lord Jesus thank you for what you did for me on the cross, paying my debt with your life. I receive that costly gift now. Thank you for being resurrected and defeating death for me. Thank you for hearing my prayer.
I welcome you as my King and as my Father. Show me how to love you, how to serve you and how to represent you as a child of the Kingdom wherever I go.

I commit to live under your guidance and follow your voice; reading your letter, your map, your Word.
I surrender to you, and ask you to open my ears. Reveal to me the ways I should go and help me to live as you will.
Enter my heart and cleanse it from all sin. Thank you, my God. Fill me now with your Holy Spirit. In the name of the Father, the Son Jesus Christ, and the Holy Spirit. Amen."

If you have prayed this prayer sincerely, then:

-God has forgiven you of all your sins and cleansed you from all unrighteousness.

Read: Jeremiah 33: 8 and 1 John 1:9

-Now God is your Father and you are his son or daughter.

His Word says that all who receive and believe in Him, become family. We are His children and He now is our Father!

Read: John 1:12 and 2 Corinthians 6:18

-You have free entrance to Heaven, to the home of your heavenly Father, when you leave this earth.

As God's child you are now an heir of His blessings and one of them is a place in Heaven. By His grace you have been justified, made righteous, cleansed from all your sin, which makes it possible to enter into the holiest place, Heaven. Not only do you have access to God now, but His Word says that He has prepared a special place for you in His heavenly home, when you depart from this world.

Read: Titus 3: 7 and John 14: 2

-You are clean and justified before God (every bad record erased), for accepting the sacrifice of Jesus in your place.

Before, our filthy garments prevented us from approaching God. Now by accepting the sacrifice of Jesus on the cross, we have been washed clean, white as snow! We have peace with God. The barrier of sin has been removed and our friendship with God has been restored.

Read: Romans 5: 1 and Psalm 51: 7

- Begin to enjoy communion with your heavenly Father.

Your Father is God, the King of Kings, and yet you don't need an invitation to speak with Him or to enter His presence. He loves you with everlasting love and is powerful, rich, merciful, generous, holy, good etc.
He desires to give you wisdom, revelations (Ephesians1:17), creative ideas (Exodus 35:31-33), healing and provision (Psalm103:2-5).

Open your heart to receive these blessings daily. Confidently draw near to Him as He draws near to you (James 4:8). In that place of intimacy you will hear Him guide you and know Him as your Helper in difficult times.

Read: Hebrews 4:16

Congratulations on your decision to begin a new life with God; the best decision you'll ever make!
Every day of my life, I realize how much His presence has sustained and blessed me.
I long for every person to understand these truths and not miss out on having a life changing relationship with God; a life of true peace, victory, and hope.

If you are already a Christian, I would like you to reflect on the following:

There are those who accept God in their hearts, but in their daily lives ignore Him, leaving the map (Bible) on a shelf unread.

Christians who live in this way (not seeking God's guidance) can easily go wrong.

How foolish it is to remain ignorant of God's will, laws and council. How many people today put confidence in their own intelligence or strength? Our natural abilities are more limited than we think.
We can do nothing of eternal value without Him. Don't wait until you've made a mess of your life to call on God. Live from His presence, His wisdom, and His Word every day. This positions you for a life of true abundance and victory!

Read: Ephesians 5:15-17

God doesn't want us to be like indifferent children who occasionally ask for help and blessing with their projects; things they planned and decided without considering His will.

When, as children of God, we ignore Him and do not take the time to know what His good will is for us, we become independent children. We drift away from the direction of our Father, exposing ourselves to traps and becoming more vulnerable to the schemes of the enemy. We wander from the safety of God's council, on to dangerous paths, and are surprised when bad things happen.

Joshua was a good leader, but once he forgot an important detail.

We read several times in the Bible that when Israel, the people of God, made important decisions without consulting or asking God's guidance, they had problems.

On one occasion, a people living in Gibeon deceived Joshua, the leader of the Israelites. This happened because he made a mistake: Before making an important decision, He failed to consult God.

(You can read this story in the book of Joshua chapter 9)

Read: Joshua 9:14

As believers, we have the privilege of personal

council from our heavenly Counselor, the Holy Spirit! (John 14:16, 26) He is with us to "teach us all things". Yet many are uninterested in what He has to say about the most important matters in life.

Many believers fall in love and marry quickly, without asking for God's guidance and wisdom. Then when trouble comes in the form of broken marriages, divided families, shattered dreams, etc., the age old question follows:
"God, why do you allow me to suffer?"
If we involve God, seek Him, and listen to the different ways He speaks, and apply all the tools He has given us to make decisions in life and love, things would be much easier and there would be less suffering.

CHAPTER 2

Do I consult God or follow my heart?

DO I CONSULT GOD OR FOLLOW MY HEART?

It amazes me when believers do not ask for or count on God's guidance.
But I am more amazed when they do not take it into account in the important and crucial decisions of life (career, dating, moving, buying property, etc.).Many make the decisions and then ask God for His blessing on them.

As a result of not seeking God's guidance in relationships (and in other areas of life), Christians experience unnecessary suffering; broken hearts, friendships lost, people leaving the church, damaged reputations, etc.

Not asking for God's guidance in life can produce frustrating results: Wasted time in wrong careers, wrong dating relationships, failed investment of personal resources, etc. Eventually after going through enough frustrations, failures and mistakes, they decide to seek the council of God.

If we would only surrender to the guidance of God and believe that He can and will guide us, many problems would be avoided!

What a joy for God and what a blessing for us, His children, when from an early age, we can count on the direction of our wise, loving, good, powerful, Father God.

Remember that your mighty and loving Father God is not too busy to hear you. He is willing and available to guide you in the way that will bring you blessing.

If you are in this category, (You are a believer but you do not seek the guidance of God), you must remember that God loves you, longs to be with you and is waiting with open arms to help you make decisions in your life and have a closer relationship with you.
Do not miss out on the guidance of a the One who created you to flourish, and knows how to make it happen!

God wants to get involved in our lives.
God loves you with everlasting love and is knocking on the door of your life to be not just a part, but to be the center of your life. He wants all of you.

He does not want to be a guest in your house, he wants to be your Father, teacher and guide. He wants to give you not just part of Himself, but all.

The Holy Spirit lives in those who receive Him. Decide today to partner with your Heavenly Guide and ask Him to open you ears to hear His leading.

Surrender to Jesus and ask Him to be not only your Savior, but your King as well. Go running into the arms of your loving and wise Father, sit on His lap every day, and begin to see the difference in your life.

Tell Him this today:

"Father, teach me your way, guide me in the straight path. I want to hear your voice. I ask your forgiveness for thinking I could do life without you and I surrender to your direction. I'm deciding today to read your letter, your word (The map: the Bible) every day and look to you in prayer; listening for your voice (To the different ways that you speak).
Thank you Father, in the name of Jesus. Amen."

Read: Psalms 27:11

Now that you have decided to surrender to the guidance of God.....

....in all areas of your life, you must:

Study the map (The Word of God).

The word of God is like a compass or a map, which guides us and helps us decide which way to go. In order not to be disoriented and lost in decision making, it is important to know the map well, so you will know what decision to make in most situations.

Study it every day, memorize it and do not forget it. Remember that it is your daily map and it is the written voice of your heavenly Father. God doesn't want us to leave His Word in a drawer, but day and night, He desires us to study it, meditate on it, and let it transform how we think.

God promises that when we receive it and follow it like an important map or instruction manual, we can walk confidently and sleep peacefully, because God will protect us from falling into traps and from evil.

Read: Proverbs 2: 1-9; 3: 21-26, Psalms 119: 44-48 and John 14:23 and 15:14, James 1:22

CHAPTER 3

Different ways God speaks to us

DIFFERENT WAYS THAT GOD TALK TO US

1 - God guides us through good council.

Read: Proverbs 12:15 and 15:22

True wisdom is expressed when we humble ourselves enough to ask for help; seeking out the wisdom of those more mature than us. Pride prevents us from receiving council. Pride says, "you know it all" or "you don't need anyone's advice". Those with a humble heart know they don't know it all.

Pride is poison. It can deprive you of what is best and create a false sense of self sufficiency; leading you to miss out on wise council in favor of your own limited perspective.

Remember not to rush into important decisions. Allow God to speak to you in different ways.
While waiting for God's "red or green light" on a certain decision, learn to listen to godly people who are mature in the faith and desire your good. Waiting can be difficult, but searching out wise counsel is never a waste of time!

Read: Proverbs 15:5

2- God speaks through circumstances

A) – God speaks through adverse circumstances due to disobedience

Example

A child and his father are enjoying a day at the zoo. The father, aware of the dangers, insists on holding the child's hand. The child refuses because he's embarrassed and doesn't think he needs protection. He wants to be free to go where he wants, without the father holding him back.

The father allows the stubborn child to walk alone, but watches closely. Suddenly, the child slips away and because of its small size, manages to squeeze through a gate where the lions are.

The desperate father, knowing the danger, looks for a way in but is unsuccessful and so he begins shaking the bars, shouting for help.

The lions have already noticed that there is an intruder in their territory and begin walking towards it. The father cannot enter and the child still does not see the danger. The child is thinking that he will be able to touch and look at the lions more closely.

The lions are approaching and begin to sniff and growl around the feet of the child! Although the lions only seem curious for now, the boy is frightened and realizes that he's in danger and begins to scream.

Then a shot is heard in the distance. Seeing that the lions are distracted, he seizes the moment, running back through the gate and out of danger.

The father hugs him and the child asks for forgiveness. After seeing that the boy was unharmed they continue their walk through the zoo. Now, the child tightly grasps his father's hand, knowing that he is safe. He can enjoy the rest of the day without fear.

Disobedience, (doing those things that God has told us not to do) can lead us to a place of peril, to a territory where the enemy can inflict harm. Wandering from the protection of our heavenly Father, makes us vulnerable.

These moments of crisis should be a wake-up call to walk again in obedience, clinging to the hand of Father God.

Jonah

A person named Jonah once found himself in the middle of a great and terrifying storm aboard a ship which was heading in the opposite direction that God had told him to go. What did the storm mean? What did this adverse circumstance mean to Jonah?

We see here, that God was speaking to Jonah through this trial. This storm meant he had to abandon that route and go in the direction God had commanded him. (You can read the story in the Bible, in the book of Jonah).

Balaam

"A person named Balaam found himself stuck and frustrated, when the donkey he was riding did not want to go any further and stopped walking. What does that adverse circumstance mean? What was God saying to him through the donkey?

This obstacle from God, meant that He was not happy with the path that the prophet Balaam had taken. So it was God himself who was standing in the way so that the prophet could not continue there.
(You can read the story in the Bible in the book of Numbers chapter 22).

In these two cases it is clear that the adverse circumstances indicated a wrong way, a "red light" from God.

Both Jonah and Balaam knew that they were going the wrong way, and that was why it was not too difficult for them to accept that they were in disobedience.

In the context of dating, an example of adverse circumstances may be as follows:

An unmarried Christian couple, having sexual relations (or unbridled romantic moments) and they are experiencing a great storm in their life. This is clearly a divine alarm, a direct consequence of disobeying God. What should they do? Change direction. Get off that path of sin.

I would ask God's forgiveness. I would set rules with my boyfriend (Not to be alone in the house, etc.) so that we don't risk temptation again. In the meantime I would begin to plan the wedding if we are in agreement on our future. But if I have no intention of marrying him, then I would end that dating relationship.

Summarizing

In short, sin (direct disobedience to what God has said) often leads you into enemy territory (Like the child inside the lion's cage).

That traumatic and fearful moment that the child endured when the lion came too close, symbolized an adverse circumstance, a direct consequence of disobeying the father.

It is like an alarm or shaking that is permitted by God, so that you understand the need to get out of that place of disobedience, ask forgiveness from your Heavenly Father, and learn to never let go of His hand.

God speaks through...

B-Uncomfortable circumstances as a result of God's protection.

Example:

A father takes his young child for a walk around the neighborhood. Suddenly a dog approaches and the boy reaches out to pet it, but the father knows this dog has a history of biting anyone who gets close. Knowing the danger, the father quickly pulls the child out of reach of the dog. The startled child cries and says to the father: "Why did you do that?" The father answers; "Sorry son, I was only trying to protect you."

Many times God will speak to us through uncomfortable circumstances. Like a good Father, sometimes He pulls us out of potentially damaging situations. He knows the hearts and thoughts of every person, therefore when someone approaches one of His children with bad intentions, if we are holding His hand, we can experience His intervention. That intervention doesn't always feel pleasant; it can be jarring, but in time we see it as a gesture of love from our Father, who was looking out for us.

Regarding matters of the heart, if you hold God's hand, seeking His guidance and protection, then when you like someone and that person has bad intentions, is a false Christian, or is not God's highest for you, He will "put the brakes" on things.

How? Usually through circumstances: Suddenly that person becomes interested in someone else, or he moves away, or does not like you, etc.

This happened to me in several cases, and it wasn't pleasant, but I also rejoiced that God took care of me and prevented a relationship that would be a dead end, or that would cause suffering. Sometimes it was just not the person God had prepared for me.

Personal example

When I was single I liked a guy, so I prayed like this:
"Dear God, if he is a true Christian and is the person you had planned for me and fits with the plans you have for my life, show me. And if he isn't, show me that too."

I remember once when I liked someone, God spoke to me through circumstances.

He gave me insight about that person. He was not a real follower of Jesus as he claimed, but a "wolf in sheep's clothing".

At first it hurt a little, but I was glad to know God was watching out for me. He helped me understand that my heart, emotions, and feelings are not the most reliable guides. When we rely on those things alone, we can find ourselves on paths we regret. It was not always easy to wait for my future husband, but today I am super grateful that God spoke to me and prevented a regrettable decision.

Conclusion

When God keeps you from a potential marriage partner, rejoice! I know that sounds strange. Rejoice? Really? Yes, because God knew something you didn't. If a trusted friend knew something about a person you were considering for marriage, something that would rightly change your mind, would you want to know? Of course.

Likewise, we can trust our all knowing Father to sort out every bit of personal information about those who enter our lives, without us knowing every detail. This should be a huge relief and source of peace when we don't see a relationship go the way we wanted. He will eventually lead you to that person who is best for you and fits the plans and purposes of your life.

Be aware of unpleasant circumstances that can be attacks from the enemy.

Example:

Imagine a well-behaved, happy child, holding hands and laughing with his Father at the park. Then, imagine the most miserable, unhappy person sitting nearby; someone who can't bear to see others happy and enjoying themselves. The old scrooge watches the joyous pair for a few minutes, then grumbles to himself, "I can't stand it anymore!" He then takes his drink and dumps it over the child's head! The poor kid is wet, confused, and no longer laughing. A pleasant day at the park is now ruined.

Of course this is an extreme illustration, (I don't know anyone mean enough to really do that), but I do know people who are resentful about the happiness of others; people who would do and say cruel things to undermine your joy.

The devil and his hosts are more than ready to do this to you. They want to cause problems, sometimes by implanting bad thoughts, false ideas, or wrong expectations, to affect your relationship with others and with God himself. What I mean is that often the adverse circumstances around you will be the product of the enemy or toxic people, who will want to steal your moments of joy; not necessarily storms that are telling us we must change direction.

In the case of Christian courtship (relationship with intent to marry) it might look like this:

Example:
You're old enough to get married and can see divine circumstances leading you to particular a person. You've been in prayer, you have not rushed, you fear God and can see that He has already spoken to you in several ways confirming that this person is for you. But a member of your family, not a Christian or maybe not a wise one, opposes that relationship. They then interfere, create problems, and bring discouragement for no justifiable reason.

In this case, I would not see that person as an adverse circumstance sent by God to stop the relationship. Rather, I would see it as the enemy's way of trying to ruin something beautiful that has come into my life; like the example of the child and father in the park.

<u>Personal example</u>

When after many confirmations I began my courtship with Steve, who is now my husband, not everything was roses.

I had several attacks from the enemy, but God's plans triumphed. The enemy couldn't stop what God had for our lives.
The devil will always want to stand in the way of our blessings, but the plans of those who have surrendered to their faithful guide will always prevail.

God speaks through...

C-Favorable circumstances and peace.

God gives confirmation of direction when, in addition to having spoken to you in various ways, you can see favorable circumstances and you have a sense of peace in your heart about it. It can feel as though a divine path has been cleared for the next step to marriage, at this specific time, to this specific person. All that is God's way of indicating a green light to take that route.

Final conclusion

We can see that God speaks to us through circumstances.

A-Adverse circumstances can arise as a result of disobedience.
Sometimes life's storms are the product of our sin and therefore we must repent and change direction.

B-Sometimes we face uncomfortable circumstances as a result of God's protection.
God sometimes pulls us out of potentially damaging situations. This "pulling" can seem unpleasant and disruptive, but is necessary.

C. Favorable circumstances.

The peace and confirmations of God are a green light for His children. When you are walking in obedience to the will of God, seeking His guidance, feeling His peace, perceiving His voice in various ways, seeing circumstances line up and doors open, it is then that God is confirming that this is the way to go.

A tool that God left us: Intelligence.

As beings made in the image of God, we have the ability to think, to reason, and make choices. We make most daily decisions using our "common sense". This basic tool helps us avoid danger and enables us to make simple decisions without having to ask what to do each time.

Read: Proverbs 2:11 and Proverbs 19: 8

There are different ways that God can speak to us, but He has also given us the intelligence to apply wisdom to various situations. When you see a car coming, you don't need a word from God to know if it's safe to cross the street. If you hire a photographer who does a terrible job, you would decide next time to hire someone else.

What about issues of the heart? For example: You notice that the person you like is dishonest, lacks respect for those in authority and treats their parents badly.

That should be enough for you to conclude that this person would not be a good husband and therefore you should stop pursuing the relationship any further.

My point is that many times knowing what to do about relationships, is a matter of applying basic moral wisdom using our God-given intelligence.

CHAPTER 4

To be guided by God you must...

TO BE GUIDED BY GOD YOU MUST ...

Know the voice of God.

As a mother, it's easy to recognize the voice of my children from others, even with my eyes closed. Why? Because I know them, they live with me and we have a close relationship.

God will speak to us in different ways so it is important to recognize His voice from others. The enemy will also try to speak to you in different ways to cause confusion.

To discern who is speaking, you must:

1) Know God first; ask Him to live in your heart.

2) Maintain a close relationship with Him.

If you are a Christian, then you have already taken step one. Now you have step two.

In order to distinguish the voice of God from others, you must have a close relationship with Him.

When you spend time with God, reading his Word and communicating with Him (praying), you can more easily distinguish His voice. If we allow too much distance or only have a superficial relationship, we never develop the familiarity of family.

Time together is a key for any relationship to grow. The more time spent with a loved one, the more we can know what the other thinks, even without a word spoken. This is true of God also. The more we are with Him, the more our hearts are connected. His desires and intentions begin to flood our own hearts and minds.

If you haven't already, then I encourage you to pursue intimate communion with God, truly seek His friendship, and go to the "secret place" to be with Him daily. Then you will find it easier to discern his voice when he speaks.

Read: Psalm 16:11

To be guided by God you must...

Get rid of all stubbornness.

To be led by God, we must be sincerely willing to follow to His direction. Many times we pray for God's guidance but we don't really want it, because we've already made up our minds. We like His direction as long as it fits "our plans".

The Bible tells us that God will teach us the way we should go, as well as counsel and watch over us along the way. But it also says this: Don't be a dummy! Well, actually it says not to be like a horse or mule without understanding. Farm animals can be stubborn. They don't know any better. But you and I are made in such a way that we can comprehend moral guidelines, think carefully, and make God-honoring decisions.

Read: Psalm 32: 8-9

Getting rid of stubbornness will also help you hear the voice of God in matters of the heart. When you like a person (or face any difficult decision) and pray for God's guidance, earnestly ask for wisdom and understanding.

Ask God to show you if that person is His best for you. Would they fit the future plans God has for you?

Then He will speak in different ways and you will realize that this person is or is not the one that God had planned for your life. If it is not, that is, if God says, "NO", accept it. Don't dismiss His direction and continue on.

When God is showing you in different ways that this is not the way to go (this is not your partner), it is better to make the break now, rather than get broken later, when there are heavier consequences.

Don't be angry with God. He is your protector. Also be careful not to let your emotions turn you into a love-sick stalker; following the person everywhere, hoping that maybe God will re-think the plan.

Just leave your future partner in the hands of God and rest in His divine providence. Focus on other things; studying, exercising, helping others, serving God, etc. Trust that in time (in God's time), He will bring into your life, that person He has prepared for you; that perfect puzzle piece. You don't have to force pieces that don't fit.

God alone has the power and wisdom to direct the paths of people to intersect at just the right time and place. As the Word says, don't trust in your ability alone to make things happen, but trust God to make straight paths for you!

Read: Proverbs 3: 5, 6

To be guided by God you must ...

Learn to be patient.

When we are faced with important decisions, it is unwise to make them in a hurry. Some choices will have implications for the rest of your life; especially dating and marriage. Patience and prayer can save you years of regret. The Bible says that doing things hastily results in error (see: Proverbs 19: 2).

When we rush into things and base decisions mostly on what we feel in the moment, we are not getting a reliable picture of the situation. We don't allow time for God to speak, guide, or confirm.

So, remember to take your time before making major decisions. Time spent seeking God's direction is never wasted.

Read: Psalms 27:14

Many young people come to God but do not know the way He speaks and guides. They end up making life choices the same way they did before becoming Christians.

They think like this:

1) I feel an attraction...

2) I see if they're interested...

3) If they're interested, we start dating...(even if that person is not their future spouse).

But we are children of God and he called us to be different; to be light and to walk in holiness. Jesus said in the Gospel of Mark that we should not act carnally or in the same way as those who are not Christians.

Read: Mark 10:43

Many people, instead of putting God's opinion first, put their own hearts in command of their decisions. No doubt you've heard the expression, "Just follow your heart!" Well, many do just that. They're quick to surrender to their desires. However, the Bible warns us that our hearts can deceive us. Emotions, feelings, and desires can be exciting and are part of being human, but they are not intended to supersede the wisdom and insight of God.

When we come to Christ, our minds should begin a process of transformation (Romans 12:2). We should leave behind old patterns of thinking, especially about relationships. Our aim should be to honor God with every aspect of our lives. This positions us to enjoy the greatest amount of blessing from Him.

Read: Jeremiah 17: 9 and Psalm 106: 12-15

Samson

(You can read the story in the Bible, in the book of Judges, chapters 13 to 16).

We read in the book of Judges that an Israelite named Samson allowed his own appetites and emotions to drive his decisions rather than the council of God. He had been set apart by God since childhood and was given great strength and responsibility. God had big plans for him.

But Samson developed a desire for women that God did not approve of; those from enemy cultures who worshiped false gods. He stubbornly gave in to these desires and suffered the consequences.

Thanks to one of his philistine girlfriends named Delilah, he was deceived and then captured by the enemy. They gouged his eyes out and threw him in prison. His life would end soon thereafter. By not obeying God's plan for relationships, Samson's entire life was wrecked, leaving his destiny unfulfilled.

Read: Proverbs 28:26

Remember then:

When you think your heart is telling you "it's love", don't rush. Wait on the guidance of God. However, if the person you think you love is not even a Christian, then there is nothing you need God to tell you because He has already said that non-Christians are off limits.

Don't make important decisions based on the feelings of a deceiving heart. Sometimes the council of wise believers can help us see what our feelings have blinded us to. Samson was blind to his heartfelt, but wrong desires.

Godly council from others and especially from the Bible can help us see beyond our feelings and make choices from a place of wisdom.

Read: Proverbs 28:26

To be guided by God you must ...

Guard yourself from bad company.

As a young person, although difficult at times, you should be careful who you hang around with. The people we call friends can influence us in ways we don't even realize at the time; affecting our decisions, attitudes, and behavior. Have you ever let someone talk you into something you knew was wrong, and later regretted it? That's the power of peer pressure. It matters who you spend time with.

Read: Isaiah 30:1

It isn't wrong to have friends who are not Christians. We can be a good influence and show them the way to Christ. We are called to be a light in the midst of darkness, so we don't need to hide from it.

However, if you see that you are not being light to them, but rather, they are leading you into darkness, then it is better to avoid that relationship, if possible. If they're classmates you can't avoid them completely.

But if you realize that their company means trouble, then do what you can to limit the time you're around them.

If you're not strong in the faith, the pressure of your friends can lead you into ways of thinking and acting that are unpleasing to God; even into sins that lead to suffering and keep you from blessings that could be yours.

Read: Ephesians 5:11

Begin today to seek out friendships with others who have a heart for Jesus and desire to please Him with their lives. If you are seeking guidance from God about your future partner, that search will likely be more fruitful if you place yourself in an environment surrounded by young Christ followers.

Example
A young man had been praying for his future wife for many years. He had a good idea of the kind of person he was looking for; someone who's character reflected biblical virtues; not perfect, but one who loved Jesus and wanted to live for Him.

One summer he was looking for a job. He didn't want to work just anywhere, but wanted to be in an environment that was good for His faith. Also, he believed if he could be around other Christians, there would be a greater chance of meeting his future wife.

Seeing that a Christian bookstore was about to open, he went there to ask for work. The pay wasn't great, but it seemed like the right place to be. That decision paid off because because one of the other newly hired employees ended up being his wife! The book--store was open for an unusually short period of time; maybe a year. A few months after this couple found each other, it closed. That couple was my husband and I!

One of the managers in charge of the bookstore wrote us a note years later, saying that she believes that place was opened just for us. The name of the store was "The Bridge". It's funny to think that God used it like a "bridge" to connect the two of us!

When you surround yourself with Christian people who share your worldview and moral values, they will not only bless your life and encourage you in your faith, but you will also be part of an environment where your future partner may be.

<u>Personal example</u>

In my teens I was part of a group of young Christians in my church, who shared my way of thinking. When my schoolmates excluded me because I didn't act like them, I wasn't affected much since I already had friends in the church group.

Read: Psalms 1: 1-3

So what I mean is that your closest and strongest group of friends should be other Christians (the church for example). This is important because we all need friends who inspire and encourage us to live rightly. At a young age you need an environment where you can develop healthy relationships, and have fun with people your age; all while growing in faith together and learning to serve God.

Read: Proverbs 13:20 and 14:16

CHAPTER 5

The protection of God

THE PROTECTION OF GOD

A great benefit of having God as a guide in the maze of life is that we have the promise of protection. God cannot be deceived, but we can. We can trust His guidance because He has the power to protect us from those who would harm us.

And since God knows the depths of people's hearts, he can protect you from those who come to you with bad or deceptive intentions.

For example, if you are searching for your future partner and seek to marry a person who is truly Christian, God can show you in some way, if that person is an authentic follower of Jesus.

Personal Testimony:

I always asked God not to let me have a boyfriend, or kiss anyone other than the person I would marry. Years ago as a teenager, I began to like a Christian boy from another city. We then started talking on the phone, getting to know each other.

In the meantime, I trusted that God would guide me.

Read: Psalms 25:3

During one of those phone calls we talked about different things but then I asked how many girlfriends he had in the past. He told me there had been several from the church; I think seven or eight. At that moment I thought, "He isn't seeking the guidance of God, but just playing with the feelings of girls. He has no fear of God and so he is not for me."

Maybe for some, my way of thinking was strict, but knowing that fact about him, I no longer felt peace. That was God's way of showing me that person wasn't for me, and so I stopped talking on the phone with him.

Today I can thank God for His care and guidance on matters of the heart. I would love for every young person to count on the blessing of having a powerful and loving Father who engages in the life of His children, for their good. God is the perfect Father; precious and loving.

When we involve Him in our lives, everything is better. The Bible says that God is our help, like a bodyguard who never sleeps. He is our best protection because He is powerful and always with us. When God is central in your life, you have safeguards to protect and free you from the traps, deceptions and stumbling stones that lie ahead.

Read: Psalm 91

We see in Psalm 91 that God promises protection to those who love and know Him. Those who accept the guidance of God and place their trust in Him, are promised to be delivered from:

The Stones:

That which may cause you to stumble in your walk of faith or make you fall into sin.

The Hunter's traps:

There are those who appear to have good intentions but may have hidden agendas, selfish motives, and may only be telling you what they think you want to hear in order to win your affections.

The Destructive Plague:

Anything which comes into your life to cause serious damage. A plague or pestilence usually starts so small that you don't even notice it. But when it grows, it contaminates and destroys more than you thought possible.

For whom is this promise of protection?

For you and for those who have said to God:

"You are my God, in you I put my hope and trust. I love you and want to know you more."

Read: Psalm 91: 2-9, 14

When you count on God for your protection, fear must flee, because you understand that not only is the best bodyguard at your side, but you also have a Heavenly army of angels that God commands to guard you in all your ways.

What a tremendous blessing we have as children of God!

Read: Proverbs 1:33

CHAPTER 6

It isn't difficult for God to bring two people together

IT ISN'T DIFFICULT FOR GOD TO BRING TWO PEOPLE TOGETHER.

Read: 1 Kings 18:1-39

If God wants to do something, He will do it despite the circumstances and against all probability. An example of this is found in the book of 1 Kings.

On this occasion the prophet Elijah gathered the people and told them to decide who they would worship; the false god Baal or the true God of Israel.

To show who the true God really was, Elijah proposed to make two burnt offerings, one for the prophets of Baal and one for him.

Then he told the Baal worshipers to ask their god to send fire and he also would ask his God. The god who sent fire miraculously, would prove to be the true God.

The prophets of Baal began to jump, shout and cut themselves in front of the altar. For hours they did this, but nothing happened.

Then came Elijah's turn. He prepared his altar and to make it even more difficult, he asked the people to dump sixteen buckets of water over the burnt offering.

Then Elijah prayed to the God of Israel. Among other things, he asked God to respond so that the people would know that the God of Israel was true and not Baal.

Then fire came down from heaven and consumed not only the burnt offering, but even the water that filled the trench around it. Then the people, seeing what happened, recognized the God of Israel as the one true God.

I want to offer two applications from this moment in history:

1) Our God is the one true God who wants us to trust and obey Him totally. He doesn't call us to a part-time relationship; going to church on Sunday but living like the world the rest of the week.

I encourage you to serve Him with all your

heart, to stand firm in your faith despite the pressure of others and you will see the difference.

2) Another thing I would like to emphasize from this story is that God is powerful and doesn't need any help if He plans to do something. My point is that when God wants to light a fire, there is no water that can stop it. When God wants to do something, He will do it, as He did for Elijah.

As for dating and marriage relationships, you can be sure that doing things God's way and trusting Him with the details, is the surest path to blessings. I made the decision to put my future in the hands of One who knows the future and I was not disappointed!

Read: Job 23: 13-14

Remember that God is the creator. He holds the universe together and is all powerful. It isn't too hard for God to arrange that meeting between you and the one He has prepared for you.

Believe and trust that God will put that person in your path at the right time and the right place. He did it for me and He will do it for you.

<u>My testimony</u>

Years ago when I first moved to Nashville Tennessee from Argentina, I remember looking for a job in a Christian business. Within a few months I found work in a Christian bookstore.

To my amazement I was hired, even though I knew almost no English. Several people worked there, among them a shy but handsome Christian guy named Steve.

At first I assumed that he wasn't for me, because he spoke English and I spoke Spanish. But as we spent day after day working together and getting to know each other, I was aware that my feelings for him were turning into something more.

However, since God had told me "No" to all the guys I liked before, I didn't even want to ask Him this time; I just figured it would be another "No".

To make matters worse, I worried myself with imaginary situations like how I would feel if he showed up with another girl one day. I thought it would be better to leave rather than end up heartbroken, so I began to look for work elsewhere, but without success.

During this time, the manager of the bookstore noticed a "spark" between Steve and I. She began trying to play match-maker without us knowing. She would find sneaky ways to cause us to spend more time together.

So the circumstances were falling into place in what almost seemed like a divine "set-up". Gradually, in different ways, God would confirm to me, that Steve was to be my husband. At first he dodged it, but then, he too realized what was happening.

When I accepted my first date with him, I already knew that he would be my husband. In fact, I said: "You don't know it, but you are going to fall in love with me and you are going to marry me."

At that moment he didn't say anything. I probably freaked him out a little. He isn't the type to reveal his emotions right away. But two days later, he told me he loved me, and soon we were talking about marriage and children.

There are too many other details, (some miraculous), to include here, but I can say that God answered my prayers and granted me the desires of my heart.

I always believed and preached the following: If we leave our search for a future partner in the hands of God, He is powerful and wise enough to do what is necessary to bring that person to us.

And don't worry about trusting God's selection. There is no reason to think He's going to match you up with someone who is your worst nightmare; a person you have zero attraction to or love for.

God loves you more than you can imagine! He is a good Father who has a good plan for your life.

He made you and therefore knows your likes and dislikes. He wants you to be delighted with the one you marry.

Trust Him. He's got it covered!

Read: Jeremiah 29:11

Why worry? You have a faithful Father.

I love what Jesus said in Matthew 6 about anxiety and worry. He told us not to be anxious or worry about the future, as if we were orphans, without a father, like the Gentiles.

He encouraged us to observe the beauty of the lilies of the field and the little birds, and realize that if God cares for them, how much more will He take care of us and provide what we need? We are worth far more to Him.

Then at the end of the passage He says that if we seek the Kingdom of God above all else, then all that we need will be provided.

Read: Matthew 6: 25-34

Remember then that you, as a Christian have the ultimate advantage: A powerful and loving Father who knows what you need and wants to give it. Rest assured: God is not going to give you a person you do not like.

He is a perfect Father who loves His children. If an earthly father knows how to give good things to his children when they ask, even more so, your heavenly Father will give you something good when you ask Him.

Instead of taking what you like without asking God, let Him be the one who chooses that person according to what He knows is best for you. He will not give you a stone. Remember that His will is not bad, unpleasant or imperfect, but it is good, pleasant and perfect.

Read: Romans 12: 2

Live happily, cultivating your friendship with God. Follow and obey His boundaries that are for your protection and benefit. Be a light to those around you and walk in the high purposes of your heavenly Father, then leave your future in His hands.

Trust that He will guide you to that person who will be a blessing and complement to your life.

I challenge you to follow this plan:

Serve God and let Him lead you. He alone has the ability to perfectly navigate every twist and turn in the labyrinth leading to marriage. At just the right time you and your future spouse will cross paths and realize there has been a wonderful divine "set up"!

Read: Psalms 37: 4, 5

The greatest happiness lies in having a relationship with your Creator and walking in the plans He has for you.

The Word of God says that in Him we are complete.

Read: Colossians 2:10

You were created to have a relationship with God (Acts 17:26, 27). As you grow closer to your heavenly Father, you realize that He satisfies the deepest desires of your soul; true contentment, joy, and happiness.

Everyone wants to be loved. People are so obsessed with finding that perfect person to fall in love with, unaware that what their heart really longs for is God.

Have you ever heard a couple at their wedding make this vow: "I promise to love, honor, and cherish you... until I find someone better...or until I get tired of you...or until my feelings change." You never hear that! What you *do* hear is the promise to be true and faithful for life, because that is the longing of the human heart.

Sadly, many married couples don't live up to their promises, but still, it is what we were made for. While people may fail, God is always faithful. He loves us with an everlasting love. Our ultimate need for perfect love can be met in Him. Seek His love first, then ask Him to lead you to a marriage partner who's greatest desire is to love you like God; faithfully, unselfishly, and for a lifetime!

Read: Jeremiah 31: 3

We long to have someone who is always willing to forgive us. When we ask for God's forgiveness, he always forgives.

Read: Psalm 103: 3

We all yearn to have someone who is with us in difficult times. God promised that when we seek Him, we will find Him and He will deliver us.

Read: Psalm 34:17

We all want someone to listen to us attentively when we speak.

God observes the righteous. He's always close and His ears are attentive.

Read: Psalm 34:15

Don't we also appreciate someone who will forget our past mistakes because they love us so much? When we ask God's forgiveness for our sins, The Bible says that He erases, buries, and never remembers them.

Read: Micah 7:19 and Isaiah 43:25

Romantic movies often send the message that if we could just "fall in love", we would always be happy, but that isn't true if you don't know God.

God is the basis of love, and without His love, there is no relationship that can provide lasting happiness. Why? Happiness depends on what happens; it can change with your circumstances. Joy, however, is deeper and it depends on Jesus.

God is the rock of the family and without Him, any wind or storm can destroy what we thought would last forever.

Anyone without God must first begin a relationship with Him, to have true peace and to fill the emptiness inside. No human being can give what we really need. Without God, there is no relationship, no amount of money, or power, or pleasure, that can satisfy our deepest hunger and thirst.

When we stop living as orphans and draw near to our heavenly Father who is waiting for us, we then find that satisfaction, that general peace and joy in life. We no longer look to other people (or relationships) to meet those needs.

Of course we can look forward to a romantic and fulfilling relationship with our future spouse. God created marriage to be amazing! He is so good and wants to give us the best, if only we will trust Him enough to follow His path and honor the boundaries He sets for our good.

Today I can say that my relationship with God has been of greater value than any other relationship.

My youth was spent without boyfriends or dating relationships and I don't regret it. It was one of my best decisions.

From an early age, I began reading the Bible, praying, and serving God. I remember the tremendous happiness I enjoyed as I served and aimed to live a life that pleased my heavenly Father. Nothing compares to that feeling of peace and joy that fills your soul.

The truth is that since we were created for a relationship with God, when we draw near to Him, and follow His ways, we discover that nothing else compares. The Father rejoices when we fulfill our purpose and we can feel His joy in our hearts!

Today I encourage you to focus on God and His kingdom because He is the source of authentic joy. When you put your future in His hands, He will not let you down.

Read: Jeremiah 29: 11-12

CHAPTER 7

Purity

Purity

We are living in a day where wickedness and sin have increased. There was a time when sexual activity before marriage was frowned upon, but now society treats it as something normal and even promotes it. As a result, we find single mothers, unwanted children, increased sexual diseases, high abortion rates, etc.

We must remember that even if the moral values of society change, the law of God, which is above society's laws, will not change.God commands us to keep ourselves pure.

Read: 1 Timothy 5:22

True wisdom is to have a proper fear, reverence, or respect for God, which includes His laws. This is "wisdom" because by following His laws we live in greater safety. It's similar to traffic laws. I may not always like having to obey the speed limit, or stop at red lights, but if we all follow the rules of the road, we are less likely to have accidents. When you decide to have physically intimate relationships before marriage, you are disobeying the laws of God. Sexual sin is like getting into a car and deciding to drive off the road. Doing that will automatically put you at risk for a "crash", hurting yourself and probably others.

Many live in fornication (sex outside of marriage), then when the "crash" comes they ask, "God, why do you allow me to suffer?" The reality is that when we do not obey the laws of God, we expose ourselves to suffering, heartbreak, and regret.

God loves us and wants to help us avoid these painful pitfalls. He really does want you to enjoy and be blessed by a romance with that special person of your dreams. That's why God designed marriage the way He did. Think of it this way: like a house with a beautiful brick fireplace. It's great to enjoy a nice warm fire in the comfort of your living room. But what if a fire started in the kitchen or bedroom? Not good. You see, fire can be a great thing...in the right context; the fireplace. God created sex to be enjoyed in a specific context also; marriage between a man and a woman. Sex outside of marriage is like fire outside the fireplace!

When people leave the boundaries of safety that God has created, having intimate relationships before or outside of marriage, they are disobeying God; missing out on His best, while inviting problems and sorrows they never imagined.

Listen to God, live in obedience, and you will see the difference.

Read: Acts 15:29 and 1 Corinthians 6:18

If you have already had relationships that led you into sexual sin, then don't condemn yourself, but ask for forgiveness and start again.

God never rejects you. He always looks at His children with eyes of love and with open arms. He knows our weaknesses, and longs to see us conquer them with His help.

If in reading this book, you have decided to listen to God, to obey and receive His guidance, then God rejoices with you. He is willing to teach you and help you live the life you were destined for; a life of victory and blessing.

A slogan Satan would be proud of: "Do what you want, as long as it makes you happy".

Do you think we will ever see that slogan painted on the walls of a police station or court of law? Probably not! Yet so many live their lives by this philosophy: "As long as it makes you happy, go ahead, follow your heart!" This way of thinking has resulted in unimaginable pain and loss for humanity.

Prisons are full of people who just "followed their hearts". Kids suffer through the divorce of their parents because someone "followed their heart" or just "wanted to be happy" with someone else. The stories are endless. But what that sad slogan really amounts to is this: "I should have whatever I want, even if others get hurt."

However, God calls His people to a higher standard. We must put the good of others first; like Jesus did. This means doing the right thing (that which God approves of), not just following our emotional impulses.

The truth is we have an obligation to do what is morally right, according to the law of God, although sometimes that will mean not getting our way or even paying a personal price.

Joseph

If you read the story of Joseph, he did the right thing by resisting the wife of his boss, who had sinful sexual intentions toward him. Joseph paid a price for refusing to give in to sin and God blessed him greatly in everything.

(I encourage you to read the full story of Joseph in Genesis chapters 37 through 39)

When you obey God, doing what is right in His eyes, even when it is costly, you will see the reward of that decision in time.

Remember, God's ways are intended for your safety and blessing.

Read: Genesis 39: 2

Don't use what you're not going to buy.

I've heard of people who go to clothing stores, pick out a dress, leave the price tags on, and wear the clothes. Then after they're done using the item, they return it back to the store. It's dishonest to wear a garment that you know you won't buy. But I think it's far more dishonest to have a boyfriend or girlfriend (The kind that you kiss and develop a bond with their family), that you know you will not marry.

When you play with the feelings of others, you are outside the will of your heavenly Father, who wants to help guide you to the person who is meant for you.

In my youth, I chose not to have boyfriends. I always thought, "I'll only kiss my husband and no one else," I prayed for that to happen, and it did. That may sound extreme. "It's just a kiss", you say. But have you really thought about it? If you are kissing (or more) someone you won't marry, then you're actually kissing someone else's future husband or wife!

I resisted the pressure of my schoolmates and

lived out my teenage years in purity and obedience to God. Looking back, I can see clearly how He blessed my life.

If you have already made mistakes in this area, don't condemn yourself, just start over and ask God for forgiveness. Tell Him you are sorry for not involving Him in your decisions, and that you will seek His guidance from now on.

We are citizens of the Kingdom of Heaven, representatives of the King, princesses and princes, so we must be careful what we do. Dating is like the first step toward marriage. So, if you do not plan to marry the person you like, there is no need to start a dating relationship.

God has given His children self-control, to submit our desires to the obedience of Christ; not allowing our emotions and impulses to control us.

Read: 2 Timothy 1:7

<u>Heartbroken but not broken.</u>

For these and other reasons, I believe dating isn't a game, but is actually the first step towards marriage. That's why I only had one boyfriend, who is now my husband.

I believe God expects this of His children; that we are to guard not only our hearts, but also the hearts of others. Deciding not to play with people's feelings by avoiding multiple boyfriends was one of the best decisions of my life. I encourage you to do the same; you will not regret it.

I'm not saying that you won't ever suffer or experience some heartache. But the reality is that it's better to suffer for doing the right thing and to have the blessing of God, than to suffer for doing wrong and to grieve the Spirit of God. (Ephesians 4:30)

The truth is, there is more suffering when you get emotionally involved with person after person, in one relationship after another.

This is because every time you end a relationship, someone will leave with a broken heart.

The more physically involved (kissing, etc.) you were with that person, the more painful the breakup. Why? Giving that kind of affection to someone is like giving a piece of your heart to them. This giving of yourself was designed for a specific context (marriage). God's design is that in marriage we can safely give ourselves completely to the other person, without fear of being abandoned.

When we listen to God, rely on His wisdom, use self-control and trust His timing, we position ourselves for blessed relationships.

Doing the right thing takes courage, because sometimes doing what is right is not easy. But setting your heart and mind on pleasing the Lord first will be what gives you the greatest chance of having the marriage of your dreams and the best safeguard against costly mistakes.

Read: Ephesians 3:13, 1 Peter 3:14, 2 Timothy 2:3 and Romans 8:17

FINAL CONCLUSION

Life is like a labyrinth. We make wrong

turns, fall into traps, arrive at dead ends, and sometimes feel lost. When it comes to finding the right marriage partner, it can seem even more frustrating and difficult, but for the Christian, it shouldn't be so.

 The journey into marriage is only one part of the "maze" of life and yet it affects so much. God knows how important it is. He cares about our marriage plans even more than we do. That's why He is always waiting to guide us; through His Spirit within, and through the "map" of His word.

As Christians, we are not lost or alone, because our God and best Friend, sees the labyrinth from above. He can point out the traps and dangers, showing us exactly which way to take.
That was the idea from the beginning; that we relate to Him and count on His help, not that we live independent of Him. Having access to these Heavenly resources along the way, made all the difference.

God really took care of me! He protected me from serious mistakes. I didn't have to go through several experimental relationships or breakups to find my husband. With God's guidance, I had only one "boyfriend"(my husband), and zero regrets!

It is possible to maintain purity while finding a marriage partner, so don't let anyone tell you otherwise. I encourage you to decide right now to live life by seeking God in all your decisions.

As you serve Him, and focus on His kingdom, He promises to give you what you need.
Trust your Heavenly Father, walk in holiness and obedience, do not be impatient.
Let him take care of the requests of your heart.
Rest in God's promises and trust that your partner is in His hands and that He will bring you both together at the perfect moment.
Having a love story guided by God is not a fairytale. It is the real love story, intended by the King of Kings for all who belong to Him. It is available for all who will seek His guidance.

CHAPTER 8

Questions & Answers

QUESTIONS & ANSWERS

How can I keep myself pure in a world that loves darkness more than the light of Jesus?

Imagine the internal struggle between the flesh (the part of you that desires ungodly things) and the spirit (the part of you controlled by the Spirit of God), as if they were two fighters. To stay pure in this world full of garbage you must nourish your spirit and it will be stronger. How?

Make time with God the most important time:

Some call it having "devotions"; Praying, worshiping, reading the Bible, even spending time in complete silence and stillness in His presence is a great way to feed your spirit and draw closer to God. Over time this becomes a holy habit, growing beyond a scheduled time of "devotions", to a lifestyle of devotion.

-Surround yourself with friends who are Christians, who encourage you in your walk and do not lead you astray.

-Do things with your time that will not make the Holy Spirit sad.

Remember that He is within you.

- Stay involved in the activities of the church. (Remember, the little lamb that walks alone is perfect prey for the lion).

-Be "light". Do good. Take someone to church. Bring flowers or a cake to some lonely person, help a neighbor, visit nursing homes, etc.

- Take care of your health. Your body is the temple of God. It's good to exercise, bike, walk, etc.

-Limit your TV hours. Avoid programs that promote or celebrate ungodly things.

-Help your parents do things around the house. (Organize the closets, clean the house, cooking, etc.)

- Keep your mind occupied with things that do not diminish your relationship with God.

- Memorize Bible verses. These truths of Scripture will help transform your mind the more you think about them. This also gives

your mind less time and attention to focus on thoughts that are spiritually unhealthy.

- Avoid conversations that do not build people up. Participating in gossip about others can diminish your spiritual health. If you are growing closer to Jesus, then you will usually sense the Holy Spirit convicting you when these moments arise. Be sensitive to this and choose to act or speak in a way that pleases the Lord.

-Think of what things you need to change. Set goals and reach them.

- Avoid spending hours on the internet looking at things that do not build faith.

-If you have enough time, help as a volunteer in the church, hospital, nursing home, etc.

To be a light that overcomes darkness in the world, we must strengthen and nourish our spirits, while denying the "flesh". That way, when the moments of conflict come, the stronger of the two will win. With the help of God you can overcome anything. Ask Him to fill you with His Holy Spirit.

Stand firm in doing what pleases your heavenly Father and don't believe those who tell you that you can't. Don't give in to social pressure. What you gain from obedience to Jesus will far outweigh anything the world can offer. In fact, when you experience God's blessings in your life, a time will come when those in the world will want to have what you have!

Read: Ephesians 4: 17-19; 5:3, 1 Thessalonians 4:3 and 7, 1 Corinthians 6:19-20; 1 Timothy 4:12, 2 Timothy 2:22

<u>*What do I do if I think I'm in love?*</u>

When you like someone:

1) Pray for God's guidance.

Go to your heavenly Father privately. Express what you feel and ask for direction.

2) First, get to know the person in the context of friendship.

Observe "from a distance". Not like a "stalker" of course. But just naturally take note of their behavior and character.

How do they treat others? Do they display godly or ungodly virtues?

You can be social without letting them know what you feel. A good rule is to treat them as you would any other friend.

No need to rush things. Emotional impulses and romantic feelings are a normal part growing up. But remember, the heart is not always reliable and can lead you astray.

3) Do not tell everyone.

Before you get married, you'll have feelings for many people, especially in the time of adolescence. I remember those times well, and I can say confidently that when you do like someone, it is wise to keep it to yourself!

It will not help to tell everyone what you feel. If you do, then you're putting yourself in potentially uncomfortable and even embarrassing situations.

4) If the feeling grows, and the other person feels the same, keep praying until you receive confirmation from God.

Seek God daily, and when you pray, ask Him to speak to you, to help you understand His will. It won't always be a "Yes". It will often be a "No" and it will hurt, but you must trust that your Heavenly Father knows what is best. In fact, you can be certain that He cares more about your future marriage partner than you do!

Read: Psalm 32: 8

<u>Example</u>

In my case, when I liked someone, if I thought they were likely to end up not being "marriage material", I would ask God to block that path in some way. The idea of getting emotionally and physically involved with a guy who would eventually marry someone else seemed foolish.

In cases like this, I trusted that God would protect me and then something always happened; maybe the guy had serious

character issues, or lost interest in me, or moved away, etc. God found a way of putting the breaks on what would've been a dead end; saving me from greater disappointment.

Also keep in mind that God expects us to show a measure spiritual maturity and responsibility. If you already know that a particular person would not make a good marriage partner, then you shouldn't have to wait for God to intervene. You need to do all you can to stop feeding those feelings and change course.

When I started to like the one who would become my husband, I tried to remove myself from that situation. Yes, I actually tried to block that path myself! But God was saying, "Not so fast!" He lovingly prevented me from finding another job so that I would be in the right place to let that relationship grow. And it did!

Then, through much prayer and patience, allowing God to guide me, He confirmed the relationship in different ways. Knowing that Steve would be my husband, I finally accepted my first date!

How reassuring to know that we have a Heavenly Guide who can still work things out for us, even when we get in our own way!

Remember, when you think you're in love:

-Get to know the person as a friend first.

-Don't tell everybody. Keep it to yourself.

-Don't make decisions based solely on feelings.

-Don't make decisions about relationships without seeking the guidance of God.

- Tell God what you feel. Ask for guidance and for protection from people with bad intentions. Ask that He speak to you in various ways. Be patient.

-When you see that circumstances are aligning and God has already spoken to you in various ways, then He has likely given you a "green light" to take the next step.

What do I do if I like someone who is not Christian?

Don't let them know how you feel. Get out of that situation. If feelings can't be controlled, the worst thing to do is keep feeding them. If this person is a co-worker or classmate, keep the interaction to the absolute minimum, but avoid it completely if possible. If they invite you out, let them know that you are not interested in a dating relationship.

What do I do if that non-Christian person I like starts going to my church because of me?

It may happen that a non-Christian boy (or girl) wants to go out with you. He invites you to go out and you tell him that you wouldn't go out with someone who is not a Christian. Then, he or she begins to go to your church. What should you do in this case?

You must wait and observe from afar. Don't get involved in a relationship just because that person came to church a couple of times. You want to be as sure as possible that this person has become a follower of Jesus before you even consider a long term relationship.

If they claim to have accepted Christ as Lord, you would be wise to allow time to inspect the fruit (Matthew 7:16). If this person has really become a believer, then like all newborns, growth must follow.

Watch as they develop other friendships in the church. See how they interact socially and notice the kind of character traits you see. Do they display Christ-like virtues? Of course you don't expect perfection, but if they lack spiritual maturity, do they at least show a desire to grow and become more like Jesus?

Perhaps you see what look like signs of real change. But be careful not to rush! You must seek God's council as well.

The fact that someone begins to go to church, claims to be saved, or does and says all the "right things", is not enough to settle the matter. Let me explain.

Many people, Christians and non-Christians, are determined to have someone they like in the church. Once they have what they want, they often stop going to church; the "mask" comes off and the "real" person is exposed. So you have to be careful and smart. Wolves and actors abound and can easily deceive you.

Read: Matthew 10:16

Personal example

Something similar happened to me. There

was a guy who asked me if I would go out with someone who wasn't a Christian, and I said no. Then he started going to church because of me. After a few months it seemed that he had changed and become a Christian! But then God showed me that appearances sometimes deceive us.

I would have told you that I was 100% certain that he was a genuine Christian, but today, I know that I was 100% wrong. He was an actor worthy of an Academy Award.

The Lord showed me that he had not changed and that clearly, he was not the person God had for me. That guy is not in the church today and I am saddened by that, but I'm thankful for God's protection from someone who was not for me and would have brought suffering into my life.

Summarizing

I do not rule out the possibility that someone who starts going to church for you will one day really get saved. It happens. Just be careful and seek God's guidance and confirmation before making an important decision.

If you find yourself in the same situation that I found myself, remember, don't let yourself be guided by appearances only, because young people can be great actors when they want something.

Always remember that people can easily deceive us, and if you want to avoid problems, it's better to seek the advice of those mature in the faith and pray for the guidance and care of your Father God.

I know of cases where a Christian married a non-Christian and the unsaved person later got saved. Why can't God do the same in my case?

Consider this: We know that seat belts can save lives. In fact, most states have mandatory laws requiring passengers to wear them. After all, they have a proven safety record. But suppose someone had a violent crash and was not wearing their seat belt, yet somehow they weren't even injured. Most people would say this was either a miracle or incredible "luck"! But I doubt it would convince you that seat belts are useless. You would be wise to keep using them.

Suppose you have a child who lets go of your hand and crosses the street without looking, disobeying your instructions. You would be thankful if they were unharmed, but you wouldn't change your mind and think; "Hmm. Maybe I was being too strict. Hey kid, just run across the street anytime without looking. I don't want to spoil your fun!"

I hope you get the point. The wise person sees the value in boundaries or laws. Laws are worth following when they have our good in mind. Just because some people cheat the law and "seem" to get away with it is a poor reason to put yourself at risk.

If God has told us not to marry non-Christians, then we can trust that His boundary or law is for our ultimate good.

Ignoring His law is like driving off the main road, at high speed, without a seat belt and hoping for the best. That's a great way to "wreck" your life.

Read: Deuteronomy 7: 3-4 and 2 Corinthians 6:14

Obeying God is always the best decision. Everything He tells us in his Word comes from love and wisdom. So save yourself the trouble and refuse to consider a non-Christian as a marriage partner.

An unbeliever typically has different moral beliefs than yours. This may not seem relevant at first, but in time these differences will show up in ways that can break a marriage.

Remember that even a marriage of two Christians is difficult and takes work, but if you marry an unbeliever, you will find yourself with problems that can be devastating. What happens when conflict arises over questions like these?
What are you going to teach your children about God?

Will your spouse allow you to continue going to church?
What if they say they don't feel "in love" anymore? Will they stay for life (like they promised) or leave you at any moment?
Can you pray together in difficult times?
What if they disapprove of you giving money

to the church?

Will they protect the marriage at all costs?

What if they start smoking, drinking, or spending time with bad people?

If a person's greatest goal is to please God in all they do, then the relationships they pursue will flourish. If God is *not* first in their life, then all of their relationships become centered around their selfish desires. This is a formula for failure.

Read: 1 Kings 11: 1-7

Remember that the foundation of a good home is achieved by building it on the rock that is Jesus Christ and modeling the love of God, which is the basis of all marriage.A non-Christian builds his life on the sand, which is unstable, and doesn't seek the guidance of God.

Someone like this will never truly be able to love you the way God intends; the way you deserve.

Read: 2 Corinthians 6:14

The moral laws of God are for our protection. Choosing to live apart from the moral guidelines that God has given us, leads to the breakdown of the family and society.

Human suffering, as well as spiritual and physical death are ultimately the result of deliberately disobeying the moral boundaries that God has established. When we disobey God, we not only miss out on His blessings but we put ourselves in unnecessary danger. It's like going to the beach and ignoring a warning flag that says: "Dangerous Waters" due to strong currents, or worse because of sharks. Getting into the water, despite the danger, with the excuse that it's hot and you want to have fun, is unthinkable. Ignoring the warnings of those who know and are there to protect, is the way of a fool.

So be glad you have a divine "Lifeguard" on the job! His warnings are not to spoil your fun. He wants you to have an abundant and joyful life in every area.

Read: Exodus 34:12 and 15

If I'm in love with someone and have a dream that seems to confirm what I feel, is that enough confirmation?

In the Bible, dreams were a common way that God spoke to people and yes, He can still speak this way today (Acts 2:17). However, not everyone has the spiritual maturity to discern accurately the meaning and source of dreams. The heart can deceive us and our emotions can influence our judgment. Dreams can be directly from God, they can be from the enemy, or perhaps influenced by your own desires. They can be a confirmation or they can be a warning. This is a complex subject that should cause you to seek out the council of a mature Christian rather than make a major decision on your own. And always remember the importance of comparing what you think a dream is saying with the standard of God's Word in the Bible.

I once dreamed that I was marrying a man with no head! This didn't lead me to believe I would marry the "Headless Horseman".

So yes, God speaks through dreams, but you are wise to ask Him to speak to you in various ways, with multiple confirmations, before starting a serious relationship.

What about direction through prophetic words?

One Sunday after a church meeting, a group of friends and I decided to stay and pray into the night.
Later on, the presence of God descended into the room and a prophetic word was given to each of us; including the name of our future husband. I don't remember all the names given, but I certainly remember mine: Esteban. I didn't run out to find every guy with that name, but kept that it in my heart.

That night God spoke through one of his daughters with a prophetic word and it was incredible. I know now that word was from God because my husband's name is Steve (Esteban in Spanish).

God cared enough about my future to send a clue, years before I met my husband. What a blessing. The funny thing is that because so many years passed after receiving that word, I actually forgot about it! It wasn't until a few years after I married my husband that I remembered it.

So do not disregard prophetic words you may receive, just be careful what you do with them. Personal prophecies don't always come with a clear time frame; some prophecy is a "now word", some will be a "future word" (like my husband's name). And just as important, because prophetic messengers are human, they are not immune to making mistakes in their interpretation of the word. Much more could be said about this subject. But for now understand this:

Prophecies can be a complement to what God is already telling us. Be open to them, but like dreams, be cautious. Test the word you receive in the light of the Word of God in Scripture. He will not lead you to do anything that violates what He's already reveled in the Bible.

Continue seeking first the guidance of God and His confirmation in other ways as well.

One additional note: There are many cases where people, based on what they feel, will say, "God told me that you are for me," but if you don't feel anything for that person, you can say, "Well, okay, but God should say something to me too, right?" If that person is for you, your heart will align with what God had planned and you will realize that this person spoke the truth.

There is no need to make personal and permanent decisions in a hurry, based on the feelings or revelations of others. You seek God and ask for His guidance and confirmation. In time, He will help you see which pieces or clues fit your puzzle and which do not. Remember, God sees from high above the "maze". Keep trusting Him.

Is it the pastors job to know if the girl (or boy) I like is "God's will" for me?

Sometimes we think it would be easier if some wise spiritual person, like our pastor, would just confirm our decision; give us a quick "thumbs up" or "thumbs down", right?

It is good to seek out the council of church leaders and other mature Christians, but we also have a responsibility to seek God by drawing near to Him. The Holy Spirit is called Counselor in Scripture for a reason (John

14:16, 26 NIV). He actually wants to council you!

But people love shortcuts. However, receiving the council of the Lord requires investing ourselves in both the study of His Word and the pursuit of His presence. God cares more about the choices you face than you do! He is pleased when you come to Him for guidance.

The responsibility for such a decision is ours. Imagine if the pastor had to fast, pray, and seek God's answer for every person who needed to know who to marry. Impossible! Don't put the burden on others to decide for you. Prayerfully consider the council of others, but ultimately, trust the Holy Spirit to confirm your path.

Read: Romans 5:5, Luke 11:9-10, John 15:7 and 16:24

Is it okay for children to have "boyfriends" or "girlfriends"?

Recently, my son, Austin, told me his eight-year-old friend already had a "girlfriend". "You gotta be kidding", I thought. Then I started wondering what age is appropriate to have girlfriends or boyfriends.

So I asked Austin a question: "If I give you the keys to the car and let you drive would you be responsible? "No," he replied.
"Right," I said. "It's dangerous because you don't know what you're doing at this age. You would surely crash. Even though I know you're eager to drive, I wouldn't give you the keys until you were ready, because my responsibility as a mother is to protect you."

I went on to explain that childhood is his time to play, go to school and be a kid, and that later, like driving, he can think more responsibly about the subject of girlfriends and dating. He seemed satisfied with that answer.

I know some parents think it's cute when their young kids talk about having a boyfriend or girlfriend at school. It may seem harmless, but we must be careful not to instill ideas in them that will create false concepts of love, relationships, and sexual behavior. Having boyfriends/girlfriends is not a game. Even young kids can get hurt and hurt others by playing with feelings.

Parents don't realize how they may even be pushing their children into sin. I can think of several examples of parents who allowed their kids to have boyfriends since childhood, and then by adolescence they were already sexually active.

So I would advise parents to let children be children. Don't give them the "keys" to things they are not ready for. That's what I told my son; "Austin, enjoy life, play ball, you can worry about all that later".

Is it okay for teenagers to go out on "dates"?

Many parents see it as normal for their children to eventually have boyfriends or girlfriends and then as teens, transition into "dating" relationships. While it is normal for kids to develop an interest in the opposite sex as they grow older, it isn't necessarily wise or safe to allow them to pursue that interest using the world's standards.

For the most part, our culture today does not view relationships through a Biblical lens.

God as creator has a design for human relationships, especially marriage. And since everything that is designed has a purpose, even our relationships before marriage have a purpose.

What then is the purpose of a "dating" relationship? ("Dating" here being understood as a romantic relationship; beyond mere friendship) What are most people looking to gain by dating? Fun? Excitement? A good time? Not being left out? Personal pleasure? etc. Alright, so...then what? What's next? Or should I ask...who's next? You see, the popular view of dating today is to find a boyfriend/girlfriend and get what you want out of that person, until someone else comes along. Dating for many today is all about meeting their own selfish needs. Who cares if people get used and heartbroken; just follow your heart, right?

However, God's ways are designed to guard your heart and the heart of the other person. You see, since we already know that His design for physical intimacy is to be in the context of marriage, then navigating the path from friendship to marriage becomes more simplified. What might that look like?

Young ladies, let's assume you've been friends with a guy for a while and know that he fits the profile of a good husband (based on principles previously discussed). You and he both sense that the friendship is becoming something more, and believe you are crossing into "love" territory. This may be the time for the next step. But the "next step" should not look like the world's distorted dating practice. In fact, to avoid any confusion, I will use a different word entirely. It's a bit outdated, but it's helpful. The word is "courtship".

It basically means pursuing a person with the purpose or intent to marry. As you both agree to move into the "courtship" phase, it is wise to set clear boundaries and a defined purpose.

Boundaries would be things that help you avoid temptations; for example: Not being alone together in risky environments, (Woman: avoid provocative clothes), avoiding physical contact that can lead to sin, etc.

Romans 5:2 is a good guiding principle; for example, guys should treat the girl as a sister, with "absolute purity", and girls treat the guy as a brother. Help each other preserve integrity in the relationship.

By defined purpose, I mean you should both agree that this courtship phase is to confirm that you both are correctly sensing God's direction towards marriage. But, because you are both imperfect people, it may turn out that one, or both of you, realize it is a mistake. Since this is a possibility, agree to set a time frame (example; 6 months) where you can both sit down and evaluate where you are in the relationship.

If you still share the same conviction about your marriage plans, then stay on course. If one of you has doubts, then maybe it's best to end the courtship and maintain a friendship. If the latter happens, then you have both conducted yourselves with honor, and can have a clear conscience before God.

Finally, I would just add that this courtship phase is something I would only allow my son or daughter to begin when they are legally of age to marry (18 yrs. usually).

Before that, I would encourage them to concentrate on healthy friendships. Group activities which include boys and girls in a safe environment can be a great way to develop healthy Christian social skills.

MODEL PRAYER FOR YOUR FUTURE PARTNER

Dear Father, I ask you to bring this person who will be my husband/wife, in your perfect time. Bless him/her wherever he/she is.

You know the hearts of everyone, so I trust you to guard me from those who would distract me from your plan.

I declare that as long as I obey and serve you, you will fulfill your promises of protection (Psalms 91) over my life.

I do not want to give pieces of my heart to all those I like along the way, but only that person who will be my husband. Keep me from making mistakes that hurt others.

Give me strength not to sin and keep me in purity, holiness, and obedience.

I trust that you will open the way for that relationship you have for me at the right time. Father God, thank you. Amen.

Hello friend.

Thank you for having purchased and read this book. If you found it helpful in any way, I hope you will take a moment and write a review or leave a comment on Amazon, so others can be encouraged by it.

Blessings!

Get other books by:

Trish Isbert Castlen

Missionary to USA /Preacher/Conference Speaker/Dr. in Theology
("Hope International Seminary of Theology")

At Amazon.com

Contact:

Email: trish.castlen@gmail.com

Facebook: Trish Isbert Castlen Oficial

Made in the USA
Monee, IL
14 February 2020

21777555R00075